Made in United States
North Haven, CT
13 October 2021

10316377R00065